JOKES FOR
THE SCHOOL BUS

Written by
Jerry Harwood

Illustrated by
Jerry Harwood and Cyndi Spence

Cover design by Jerry Harwood

Website
www.ajokebookforkids.com

To Jake, Hope you like this Book !

www.bookstandpublishing.com

Jerry Harwood

Published by
Bookstand Publishing
Morgan Hill, CA 95037
3234_5

THIRD EDITION

ISBN 978-1-58909-819-0

Printed in the United States of America

Contents

A JOKE BOOK FOR KIDS

JOKES FROM THE SCHOOL BUS

JERRY HARWOOD - AUTHOR

website - a jokebookforkids.com

Foreword

For

Jokes For Kids From The School Bus

Written by:

Dave Maher, principal of St. Paul School
Florence, KY.

Driving a school bus involves a little science, a little bit of patience, a minimum of ignorance, and mostly, a lot of creativity. In any other job involved in supervising kids, are you ever required to look in the opposite direction of where they Are, and at the same time keep them under control?

Jerry Harwood, driver of bus 185, has found the answer---- jokes--in the form of riddles. All kids, even adult ones, love jokes. And contrary to popular opinion, the simpler they are, the better. Jokes are a way of interacting that keeps kids occupied and out of trouble.

The present volume contains lots of jokes. Some are good; some are groaners. Most kids like the groaners the best. Jerry and His students have been telling jokes that are riddles for years. He has decided to write them down for our groaning enjoyment. Sit back, relax, and pretend that you are a 10-year-old, 4th grader again. You are sure to enjoy, and you'll be home before you Know it.

Dave Maher
Principal
Saint Paul school

Snowman Jokes

What do you call a snowman hobo?
A snow drifter.

What does a snowman eat for breakfast?
Frosted flakes.

What does a lady snowman use to fix her hair
when she gets up in the morning?
A snow blower.

What is a snowman's favorite sport?
Snowball or snow boarding.

What does a farmer snowman use on his farm?
A snowplow.

**What's the first thing a snowman does
When he gets up in the morning?
He takes a snow shower.**

**When a little snowman can't ride a tricycle, what
does he ride? He rides an icicle.**

**What do you call a snowman who is
a little goofy? A flake.**

Where is the snowman championship
football game played?
The snow bowl.

Where does the snowman prince take the
snow lady princess to dance?
The snow ball.

What does a snowman wear
When he dresses up?
A snowsuit.

What does a snowman wear when he's in
the mountains? A snowcap.

What did the snowman say when the boy said
"thank you"? It's snow problem.

What do you call it when a snowman lies to you
about how nice you look, how smart you
are, and how much he likes you?
A snow job.

On what day does a snowman show up at school?
A snow day.

What would you have if one snowman bit
another snowman? A frosty bite.

When someone said to the snowman comedian,
that's not funny. What did the snowman say?
It's snow joke.

What is a snowman's favorite carnival treat?
A snow cone.

Where does a snowman keep his money?
In a snow bank.

What does a snowman use to fix his hair?
A snow comb.

What is working in the snow like?
It's snow fun.

What did the snowman whisper to
his bride during his wedding?
I think I'm getting cold feet.

What did the sheriff say to the snowman
When he arrested him? Freeze!

What did the snowman say when someone
asked him if he wanted a drink? Snow thanks.

Animal Jokes

**What insect is very self-confident?
A cocky roach.**

**What did Dr. Duck, the psychiatrist, say to the pond?
You have deep problems.**

**What did the pond say to Dr. Duck?
You're just a quack.**

**A duck went to the baseball game, and a "fowl"
ball was hit right at him. What did the
batter yell to the duck?
Duck!**

What did the tiger say to his deer friend?
I'd like to have you over for dinner.

After the tiger finished his dinner, what did he
say to his deer friend? Catch you later.

What did the tiger say to his deer, sweet friend
after dinner?
I'd like to have you over for dessert.

What did the tiger say to the zebra?
Nice stripes.

What fish is the easiest to fool?
The sucker fish.

Why does a fish always know how much he
weighs? Because he always carries
his scales with him.

Where does a tired fish sleep?
In the creek bed.

What did the moose say to the
bear during the snow storm?
I can bear-ly see you.

How did the little bear cub catch a cold?
He went outside in his bear feet.

Why did the animal lover buy the new car?
Because it had a car-pet.

Does your dog bite?
Only if you are delicious.

What did the bee say to the flower?
Hi honey.

When the little bear cub misbehaved, what
did his mother threaten to do?
Spank his bear bottom.

What is the perfect name for a lady turtle?
Shelley.

What did the deer say to the honeydew melon?
How do you do honeydew.

What worms make a hearty meal?
Grub worms.

Why did the squirrel act nutty?
Because he wanted his girl friend to like him.

Why did the cat eat the rat?
Because the rat was fat.

What did the flower say to the bee?
Buzz off.

Why was one squirrel chasing another Squirrel?
Because the first squirrel was acting a little nutty.

What is the favorite food of a
patriotic mouse? American cheese.

What is the dog Fi-doe's favorite snack?
Fi-doe likes pie doe.

What did the kitty cat say when he was put Into
a cage? Let meee ouuut!

What is a catalyst?
A list of the names of all your cows.

What do you call a salt block in a
cow pasture? A cattle lick.

What do you have when your chubby dairy cow has
short legs? Low fat milk.

Why did the rabbit not like the barber?
Because he heard that the barber is
always cutting hares.

What's the difference between a lolly-pop and
a lolly-pup? The lolly-pup licks you.

Why did the werewolf not have mirrors in his
house? He did not want his problem to reflect
badly on his family.

What do you get when you cross a bunny with
a shellfish? A shellfish bunny that
won't share his carrots.

Where does an oyster sleep when it's tired?
An oyster bed.

What insects do your mom and dad want
you to always carry with you?
A (bee) nice, (bee) careful, and
(bee) good.

Shoe Jokes

What shoes never work? Loafers.

Why didn't the shoe go to heaven?
He lost his sole.

Why didn't anyone like the shoe?
They thought he was just a heel.

Why did the shoe get detention in school?
Because he stuck
his tongue out.

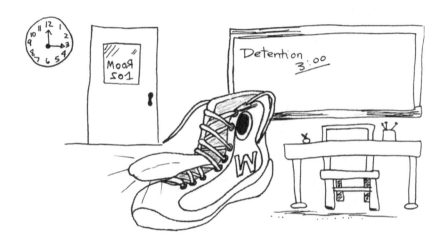

Why did the shoe gag?
He had a sock stuck under his tongue.

What shoe flies to work, flies to vacation, flies everywhere? Just a plain shoe.

What kind of shoes do you keep tied up in the back yard? Hush puppies.

What shoes are always changing their Stories? Flip flops.

Why was the shoe late for her date?
She was tied up.

What shoes see the most luv?
Tennis shoes.

Why was the shoe salesman afraid to go to work?
He was afraid his boss was going to
give him the boot.

State Jokes

What state reminds you of a small drink?
Minni-soda.   (Minnesota).

How did the state of Mississippi get its name?
Mr. Sippy took a wife, and she became known
as Mrs. Sippy   (Mississippi).

How did the state of Michigan get its name? A man
and his wife lived in the territory. He was a truck
driver, and his name was Gan. Once when he was
about to leave on a trip, his wife said "I'll
(miss ya Gan)" (Michigan).

What state is like a paved path surrounded
by water? Rhode Island.

What state's name means sick and loud?
Ill-in-nois - (Illinois).

What state sounds like something that describes a
bad feeling? Misery - (Missouri).

What did the university of Utah fan say to the
college basketball center? You tall - (Utah).

Where did Diana's mother put Diana's
favorite dessert? In-diana - (Indiana).

When the fashion designer came to pick up his new
girl friend Dela, what question was on his mind?
What will Dela-wear? - (Delaware).

On Halloween night, Mary, the witch, flew over
some of her friends. What did they yell to her?
"Mary-land"   "Mary-land" - (Maryland).

What state sounds like the ability of a
bad child to talk back?
Can-sass. (Kansas).

A man did not make a lot of money, and he had a lot of debt. What did he say about it, and in what state did he live? I-owe-a-lot - (Iowa).

What state has sounds that are like a religious ceremony, a cold symptom, and a group of things that go together?
Mass-achu-setts - (Massachusetts).

The bank teller was excited when he was given a one hundred dollar bill, but he accidentally cut it Into two pieces. He then asked if anyone had some tape, why? Because he was going to connect-d-cut - (Connecticut).

A boy was born in America, and he liked all the states, but he was born in one particular state so what state was that?
His "(Maine)" state.

A western state whose first part is not black and white, the second part is a math process, and the third part is an exclamatory word.
Color-add-oh - (Colorado).

A state that is spelled like the description of an empty gold mine. Ore-gon - (Oregon).

A man named oming was questioned, by his wife about no gift, on her birthday.
She said, " why-oming?" - (Wyoming).

What state could be part of a new sports uniform?
(New Jersey).

What state makes you think of a carpenter?
Art-can-saw - (Arkansas).

What states have a lady's name?
(Virginia and Georgia).

What state sounds like a new puppy?
A new Yorky - (New York).

What is a horse's favorite state?
Neigh-braska - (Nebraska).

What state has a first syllable that is a man's name,
the second syllable means to fold in, and the third
syllable is the postal abbreviation for that state.
Ken-tuc-ky - (Kentucky).

What state can you remember by looking at your
pencil? Pencil-vania - (Pennsylvania).

Oh smith fell asleep in the woods. When one of his
friends took a short cut through the woods, he
tripped over oh and woke him up.
What did the surprised friend say?
Oh! Hi, Oh. - (Ohio).

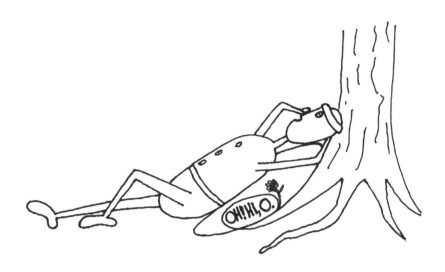

A girl named Flori had a brother who was not too
smart. Some of his friends thought he didn't even
know his sister's name, or the name of the state in
which he lived. When they
asked him, What did he say?
Flori-dah! - (Florida).

Scary Jokes

What is a ghost's favorite shop?
A pet boo-tique.

What did the baby mummy say when he got hurt?
Mummy, mummy, mummy.

What do they say about a mummy
that's a Little crazy?
He's not wrapped too tight.

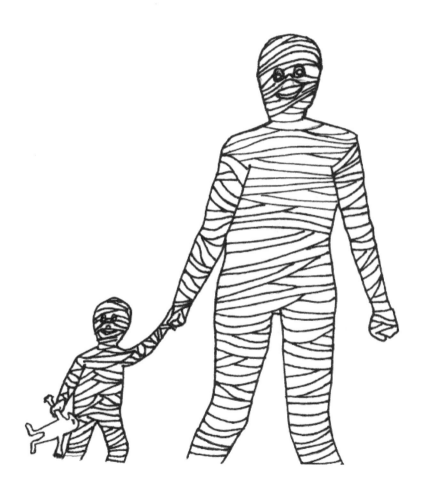

Where does the mummy's baby sleep?
In the baby crypt.

What do you call a pumpkin that's not too nice?
A jerk-o-lantern.

Mr. And Mrs. O'lantern had a baby boy.
What did they name him?
Jack -- Jack-O-Lantern.

What do you call a pumpkin that
keeps you laughing?
A joke-o-lantern.

What do you call a country
jack-o-lantern's relatives?
Pump-ken folk.

How could the witch afford to buy anything she wanted? She was weally, weally wealthy.

What kind of footwear do ghosts wear on Halloween? Boo-oots.

During our cook out on Halloween, guess what we are going to grill? Hollow weenies.

Mr. And Mrs. Monster had two baby boys what did they name them? Frank and Stien.

Why did the kid take cough drops to the funeral home? Because of all the coffins.

Why did the ghost not go to the dance? Because he had no body to go with.

What did the ghost send to his ghoul friend? A boo-quet of flowers.

Why do you think a witch is such a good student
in school? Because she is a great speller.

Mr. And Mrs. Loween were married and they
had a baby boy. What did they name him?
Hal ----- Hal-loween.

How did the witch know when it was time for
Halloween? She checked her witch watch.

What does the mother witch say to her little witch?
Clean up your broom.

Why did the bats go to the baseball game?
Because they heard that bats are
necessary to play the game.

Why did the old vampire with no teeth stop by
the fast food restaurant?
He needed a straw to suck your blood.

Why was the little vampire picked up
late at night by the police?
Because he was out after curfew.

Ordinary Jokes

We made so many jokes, it's snot funny.
Yes, we did!

What do you have when a jerk falls down in the
mud on the side of the road, rolls across the road,
and then rolls back across the road?
A dirty, double-crossing jerk.

How do you know that trains like chewing Gum?
Because, all they want to do is choo-choo-choo.

What do you call a crazy person with a coke?
A coke -n- nut.

A man traveled all the way around the world
and then fell. What would you call that?
A long trip.

Why did the tree go to the dentist?
He needed a root canal.

What wood misbehaves the most?
Knotty pine.

Who is the tree's favorite action figure?
Stickman.

Why do you go to school?
So you won't be a fool.

A circus plane was flying a circus to South America, but it crashed in the jungle. Cannibals captured and ate everyone in the circus except the clowns. Why did they not eat the clowns?
Because clowns taste funny.

What did the kid say to the clown with a tear in his eye? Can't you take a joke?

Two flowers were riding a bicycle built for two when a bee spotted them. What did one of the flowers say to the other one? Petal- faster!

Where does a flower sleep?
In a flower bed.

What bird flies to Hollywood? The starling.

What is the only bird that can carry a tune?
A humming bird.

Why did the bird go to prison?
Because he was a robbin'.

What bird would feel comfortable in
a catholic church?
A cardinal.

What is the saddest bird? The blue bird.

What is a bee's favorite bird? A buzz-ard.

What do you call a pigeon that sits at the bar?
A stool pigeon.

Thanksgiving is getting close, why should you be
careful? Because some people may not
yet have their turkey.

Why should you never invite a turkey to dinner?
Because he will gobble down everyone's food.

What did the pilgrim say to the turkey on Thanksgiving Day? It's my turn to gobble.

What did the pilgrim find out on Thanksgiving Day? The turkey is not the only one who gets stuffed.

Why should you not eat too much on Thanksgiving? Because you don't want to get stuffed, and look like a turkey.

What did the turkey say when the pilgrim asked him to stay for dinner? No thanks, I'm stuffed.

What does a kid who drops out of school drive?
A loser cruiser.

Why did the driver take his car to the tire shop?
Because his car's wheels were old and
needed to be retired.

When a car is in a wreck, where does it
have to go to get checked out?
To the dent-test.

Four people were riding in a car to work.
By the time they got to work, they
were soaking wet, why?
They were in a car pool.

What did the nose say to the boy?
Why are you always picking on me?

Why did we stop laughing at our snotty jokes?
Because they're just snot funny.

What kind of flowers grow between your nose
and your lips? Forget-me-snots.

That snot funny. No it's snot.

What did one nose say to the other nose?
Why are you being so snotty?

When is staying home from school, snow fun?
On a surprise snow day.

What's a joke like, that's made up
by a sick kid?
It snot a funny joke.

What tree has the worst personality?
The old crabby apple.

What did the door say to the wide open window?
Shut-up!

If you go to a yard sale, and you buy one - how
do you get it home? A dump truck.

When you're fixing up your house what's
the fastest item you can use?
Thinned paint - it runs.

What did the painter say to the thin paint?
You drip!

Why did the girl want a new pair of glasses?
Because she wanted to look good.

Why was the light bulb such a good student?
He was very bright.

What do you call meat that doesn't work?
Meat-loafer.

Why does everyone want a blonde when the lights
go out? Blondes are light headed, and you can see
in the dark when one is with you.

How do we know that all sponges go to heaven?
They're holy.

Where do you find the best joke tellers?
At the joke bank.

Why did the little fish not show up at school?
Because he was caught playing hooky.

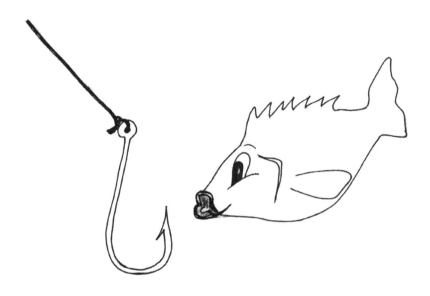

What can you give away, but still keep?
A cold.

What do you call an astronaut who is a little silly?
An astro-nut.

What do firemen put in their soup to make it hot?
Fire crackers.

What do you get when you send your french
fries to the beauty shop? Curly fries.

What do you get when you cross a
man with a bean?
A human bean.

What do you call a person who takes all the boxes
of cereal out of the cabinets in the kitchen and
destroys them? A cereal killer.

What's your name? Can you spell it? i–t, it.

**Why did the kid stop surfing channels and the net?
Because he was surfing bored.**

**What do you have when the letter T falls
into your shoe? A "t-shoe."**

**What does a snotty w and y want between them?
A clean-x.**

**What did the grandmother say when her
granddaughter tore a hole in her sweater?
Darn it!**

**When the kid went to the department store,
why was he not able to buy a DVD?
Because, he was in the "BVD" department.**

Why did the school personnel manager know
that he should not hire the lady who was
applying for a cafeteria job? Because
she said, "I do not knead the dough."

What's the difference in a cul-de-sac in the
summer and in the winter? In the winter, it
Is a colder-sac.

Why was Will afraid to go into battle with his army
buddies? Because his commander was always
yelling, "Shoot at will."

What is the favorite amusement park ride
in the city?   The mayor -go-round.

Santa does not visit bad kids or kids with colds,
why?   Because one is naughty and
the other is snotty.

Why was Mrs. Clause jealous of Rudolf?
Because Santa was always calling him deer.

Why did Santa think Rudolf had a cold?
Because, his nose was red.

Why were all of Santa's helpers depressed?
Because they had low elf esteem.

What candy can help you if you need
help walking? Candy canes.

The Latest Jokes

**How do pirates help their country?
They join the ar-r-r-r-r-rmy.**

When you look out on your lawn, and see two weeks worth of newspapers, how does that remind you of cable television movies? Pa-per view.

Why was the school bus driver late picking up his kids? Because when he tried to wake up the school bus, the bus didn't want to get up, so It turned over, then went back to sleep.

What do you call toys that belong to a boy that never takes care of them? Toys-r-rust.

What did King Arthur call the sleepy knight?
Sir Snores A Lot.

What did the lighted light bulb say to the
unlighted light bulb? Lighten up.

How did one light bulb know the other light
bulb was not too smart? It was clear
that he was not very bright.

What did the minister say when he saw
a fire in the church? Holy smoke.

What fish goes well with a peanut butter
sandwich? A jellyfish.

What does a happy wrapper make?
Glad wrap.

**Why did Santa Claus change clothes on
Christmas eve?
Because it was time for his date.**

**Santa has snow deer, why?
He traded in his rein-deer.**

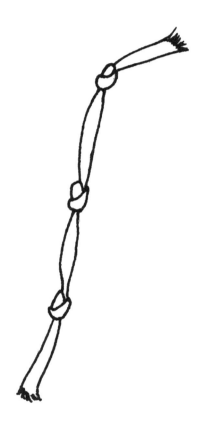

**Why didn't the string get anything for Christmas?
Because he was too knotty.**

What candy is the easiest to trick? Suckers.

What did the house say to the wind
after the storm?
You blew it.

Why was there no sundae at the restaurant
this week?
Because they were out of Ice cream.

When the mom and dad's little boy was born,
he was very smart and also rude.
So what did they name him?
Aleck ------ smart - aleck.

Why was the cowboy afraid to be around the art teacher? Because the art teacher was always saying, draw!

What do you call a girl who was named after the creek?
Brook.

Who delivers Easter eggs to the anesthesiologist on Easter? The "Ether Bunny."

What is the name of the year in the life of a person when she weighs the least?
A light year.

Mr. And Mrs. Mist wanted a scientist in the family.
They had a baby girl.
What did they name her? Kim - - - Kim mist.

What would you call a period of time when a
record number of frogs were hatched?
Leap year.

What's the wimpiest candy?
Suckers, because anyone can lick them.

Cats don't eat insects so why was the cat so interested in the ant that was walking down the middle of the highway?
Because cats do eat (road-ants).

What amusement park ride did the couple ride on their honeymoon? The marry-go-round.

What is the bravest sandwich?
A hero sandwich.

What is going to school on a snow day like?
It's snow fun.

What did the snowman say when the boy ran
into him with his sled? It's snow problem.

Once there was a real estate agent who was afraid
of bugs and storms. What day was he most afraid?
The day he saw a house fly during a tornado.

Why did the barber go to jail? Because he made
too many short cuts - on his taxes.

Why did the third grader go to detention?
His teacher was helping the class learn their
spelling list. She said " Ok Jimmy, I'm going to
give you two of the spelling words, and you use
them in a sentence. She gave him (teacher and
glee). Jimmy thought for a while and then he
said, " my <u>teacher</u> is uhh--- uhhh – <u>glee!</u>"

Why was the school bus driver, who wanted to
keep the bus quiet, happy to see the little girl
back on the bus after her operation?
Because, She had her (add – noise)
(adenoids) removed.

Mr. And Mrs. Powder had a new child, what did they call him? (Baby) - Baby Powder.

What did the kitty cat mail to his friend? A kitty letter.

Why was the kitty cat arrested? He was kitty littering.

**What do you call a bee that can't speak well?
A mummble bee.**

**When the boy grabbed the bag of chips,
what did one chip say to his friend?
Look out, he bites.**

**What do you call it when a boy horse dreams
about his girlfriend? A night mare.**

If water could be an athlete, what kind of athlete would it be? A down hill runner.

What is the name of the newspaper that is read by the rainbow trout and all his friends who live in the mountain stream? Current events.

What do you call a kitty cat that is afraid
of its shadow?
A scaredy cat.

**Why is driving on a street with a lot of
potholes like being in church?
It's a very holy experience.**

**Why wouldn't the shoe work?
It was too lacy.**

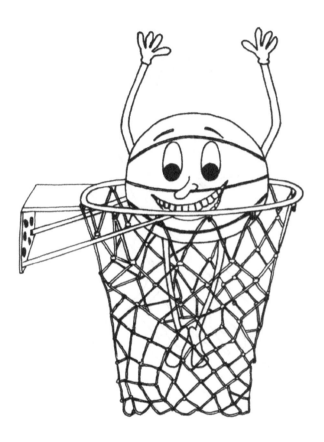

**What did the basketball say to the hoop?
Look out, I'm coming through.**

Where does a naughty gnat live?
Sin-sin-gnati – Cincinnati.

Where do the coolest animals live?
The North Pole.

Ot, the little carrot asked his father,
" Why don't kids care for me dad?" Dad said,
" I don't know, but I care, Ot."

Why are ducks always so sleepy in the afternoon? Because, they're always up at the quack of dawn.

Where do you find the best lollypops?
At the licker store.

Is there life on Pluto? Yes, fleas.

What pies should you never have for dessert?
Cow pies.

Why did Tennessee coon hunters want to
vacation in Mexico? Because they heard
Mexico had canned coon.

Why was the honeybee embarrassed when he
saw Mother Nature in the spring? Because
he saw her bloomers - flowers and trees.

**What do you call a dinosaur that
has no teeth? A gummy - saurus.**

**What did the little kangaroo's mom say to him
on his birthday? Hoppy birthday.**

**Why did the clown go to the doctor?
Because he was feeling just a little funny**

What did the booger husband say to his loving booger wife? "You are my sugar booger."

A boy muskmelon was trying to talk his girlfriend into running away and getting married, what did she say? She said, "No, we can't elope, cantaloupe."

**What do most kitty cats like for breakfast?
Shredded tweet.**

**What is the most dangerous pedestrian in
the alphabet? The J-walker.**

**What did the tick say to the dog?
I'm stuck on you.**

71107289R00051

Made in the USA
San Bernardino, CA
11 March 2018

CPSIA information can be obtained at www.ICGtesting.com
Printed in the USA
LVOW01s0347091213

364417LV00002B/9/P